classwise

Organisation and topics throughout the infant school

Kathie Barrs and Katie Kitching

Our Puppet Sand Pit!

Illustrated by Kathie Barrs

First published in 1990 by
BELAIR PUBLICATIONS LIMITED
P.O. Box 12, Twickenham, England, TW1 2QL

© Kathie Barrs and Katie Kitching

Series Editor Robyn Gordon
Designed by Richard Souper
Photography by Kelvin Freeman
Typesetting by Florencetype Ltd, Kewstoke, Avon
Printed and bound by Heanor Gate Printing Limited

ISBN 0 947882 13 8

Acknowledgements

The authors and publishers would like to thank the children and staff of Orleans Infants School, Twickenham, Richmond-upon-Thames, and Buckland Infants School, Chessington, Kingston-upon-Thames, for their generous support and contributions during the preparation of this book.

Contents

Organisation

The Integrated Day

The key to an integrated day is organisation and planning. The classroom needs to be arranged with this in mind, making sure that equipment and materials are readily available and easily acquired by the children.

RECEPTION AND YEAR 1

When the children first come into school the classroom should be organised along the lines of the nursery, with well-thought-out purposeful play activities available. The children come into school, often accompanied by a parent, and can immediately be involved in a meaningful activity, with an adult for interaction. This gives the teacher time to greet the children quietly and calmly, to speak to individual parents and to deal with any problems that may arise, such as with children who find difficulty in settling.

It is valuable to have meetings with parents to explain the importance of a well-planned 'play activity' approach to learning and why this method has been adopted.

The children will need to be prepared for a true integrated day: early goals should be attainable – consider planning a child-centred 'mini-topic' designed to last a short time. 'Newness' might be a suitable beginning – the children are new to school, they may have new clothes especially for school, there are new books and pencils etc. A display of old and new toys could be assembled, and a gallery of 'new people' (self portraits) might form a wall display. This mini-topic will give the teacher time to assess and record the abilities of her/his new intake. Other mini-topics could be: ourselves, my face, my friends, I am at school, etc.

It is worth taking plenty of time to explain the 'rules' of the classroom; why certain areas are for a restricted number of children, how to put on aprons, how toys are stored, and so on. There should be sound reasoning that the children understand and appreciate behind the class rules.

Later, when children have become accustomed to the classroom environment, it will be possible to organise the day in a more directed way. The class should be grouped flexibly in mixed-ability groups, possibly based on friendship, and each session must be carefully planned with all equipment and materials ready. Some activities will have been covered in earlier sessions and will be familiar.

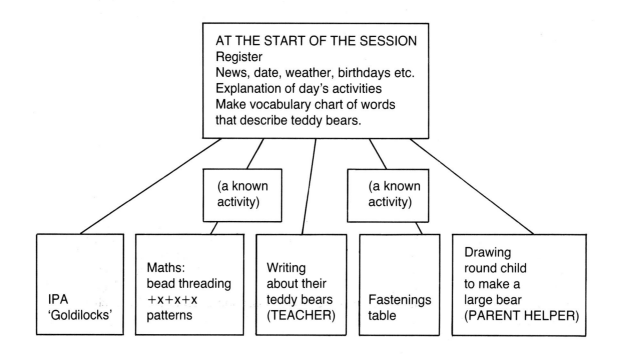

If an adult helper is not available the teaching group could be given a simple task such as drawing their teddybears while the teacher provides the support needed for starting the large bear pictures, before returning to the teaching group. All materials must be ready. The teacher and parent helper could also pay attention to the 'fastenings' activity as this may require support.

Depending on the daily routine, the groups can circulate the various activities with discussion periods in between. When planning the order of activities, the teacher needs to take into account the value of the sequence, e.g. language following imaginative play, and static activities following active.

How far the integrated day is developed in Year R and Year 1 will depend on a number of factors:

The children's previous experience, e.g. nursery, catchment area etc.

Philosophy of school/L.E.A.

Number of children in the class.

Sequence of admittance to school, e.g. into existing groups, part-time, summer intake, etc.

Remember that young children have short concentration spans and are easily distracted: try to make activities simple, but interesting and effective, and always have sound intentions. You should have a large collection of simple songs, poems, counting rhymes etc. It is useful to have a notebook for these. Good beginning sources are: *This Little Puffin* compiled by Elizabeth Matterson, and the *Puffin Book of Nursery Rhymes* by Iona and Peter Opie – and don't forget other teachers!

YEAR 2

When the children first start in the top infant class, there is obviously a need for a certain amount of continuity from their previous year. By the end of their final year as infants the children should be establishing more independent work habits, taking responsibility for the completion of tasks directed by their teacher. This could be aided by individual or group 'Work Charts' to act as a check list for completed tasks.

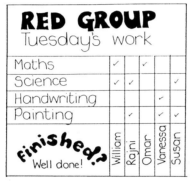

A system of stickers or, where necessary, a personal 'Comment Sheet' could be incorporated, allowing the child to make a note of the tasks he/she enjoyed, found difficult, was pleased with etc.

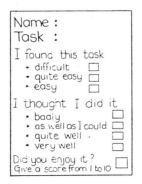

The beginning of the working day is vitally important for setting the tone, and establishing the intended tasks. After the initial registration and 'chatting' period, the teacher needs to explain carefully what is involved in the day's activities. Failure to ensure that all the activities are fully understood could result in queues of bewildered children interrupting the teacher's group, asking what to do next! A flow chart for the children's use solves the problem of their knowing which job to move on to, and helps to prevent overcrowding at the most popular activities. Although the children start the day with their own group (preferably not ability based), they are free to move to their next job when they are ready, without having to wait for the rest of their group.

If the groups are named after colours, the tasks on the flow chart can be written in those colours, thus telling the children which job their group should start with. As they work their way through the chart, the teacher is free to call together flexible groups of children to work on specific tasks with close teaching and supervision from him/her.

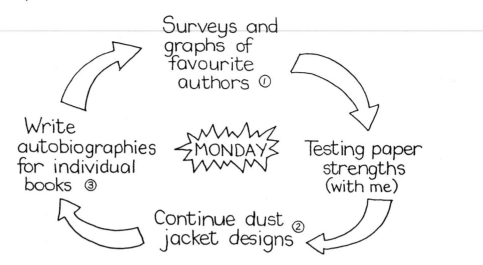

As there is usually a selection of equipment accompanying each activity it is more efficient for the children to move around the room, doing their work in the relevant areas of the classroom. Ensure that there is a plentiful supply of writing materials in each area, and that vocabulary cards are readily available.

A system needs to be devised whereby the worksheets, if any, for each task are clearly stored for the children to help themselves. A shelf with shallow boxes or trays, labelled with numbers corresponding to numbers on the flow chart, makes it easy for them to find the relevant paperwork.

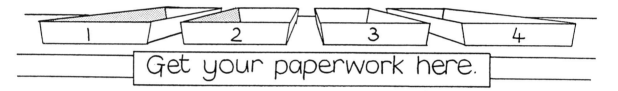

There also needs to be a 'Finished Work' drawer or tray for the completed sheets or books.

At the end of the session or day, a 'coming together' time on the carpet serves to bring the children back to being a member of a class to find out what everyone else has been doing. It is also an ideal opportunity for speaking and listening skills to be practised.

With experience of the class, the teacher will come to know how long particular tasks will take to complete – if necessary, one group of activities can be extended into the next day, should the majority of children not have finished. For those who do complete their work, and perhaps require extension, there could be a range of enjoyable, investigative activity cards for them to progress to. It is also helpful for the children to know what they are permitted to get on with, while the rest of the class are still working.

There should also be a range of additional tasks available, many of which apply across the infant age range:

Calculator games
Colouring sheets
Plasticine cards
Crossword/word searches
'Bits and Pieces' books
Tracing pictures
Song sheet folders
Individual topics
Puppets and play books
IPA (if free)

Maths/Science areas (if free)
Construction toys and task cards
Magnifying glasses
Sewing activities
Jigsaws/board games
Sequencing activities – Maths and Language
Clipboard activities – questionnaires
Computer (if free)
Selected board games

Looking at the classroom

It might be useful to take an objective look at the classroom and consider some of the following points:–

Is the space in the room used to maximum advantage? Many classrooms have problem areas – size, position of door/window/sink; lack of storage space etc., but with careful planning most can be arranged to provide a good working environment.

One point to keep in mind is the need to have space for the children to line up when necessary.

Can the furniture be arranged to create several clearly defined working areas?

If space allows, some teachers like to have a chair for each child – these could include those in the working areas.

Can children move freely round the room without interfering with others? Are 'quiet' areas (e.g. reading/listening) situated as far as possible from 'active' areas (e.g. sand/water)? It would be preferable to have the sand/water adjacent to the Maths/Science area, Art near the sink etc.

Is there furniture which is not used to full advantage? Consider adapting furniture, e.g. legs on a table shortened to bring it to children's level; doors removed from cupboards to provide easier access; a pinboard attached to the back of a bookcase or shelving unit (remember to check with the headteacher before adaptations). A coat of paint may improve the appearance of a piece of furniture – parents could help with this.

Can you use space outside the classroom – for example, corridors? Don't forget, however, that others use these communal areas, so avoid obstructions – *in particular making sure that fire door exits are not blocked.*

Window ledges are useful storage areas – wire shoe racks no longer needed in the cloakroom could be used on the sills. Avoid blocking too much daylight.

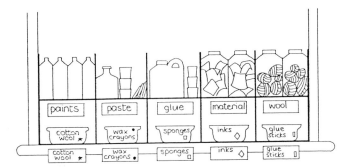

Is it easy for the children to take out and put away equipment and toys? A motif or silhouette on the shelf might aid organisation.

Perhaps toys could be kept in two or three separate areas so that at tidying-up time there isn't a crowd in one particular place.

Pinboards are often placed high on the walls – is it possible to use a space lower down? Consider placing a table in front so that the display area can include objects/plants etc. Don't forget the space under the table for covered boxes (see photograph page 13) containing paper/newspaper/fabric etc.

Ensure that displays are well presented, with clear captions, and that they are relevant to work going on in the classroom.

Accidents are inevitable. Can the children reach and use 'cleaning-up' equipment? Have these readily available:

− a broom (with shortened handle – full length may cause a further mishap).
− dustpan and brush, hanging from cup hook situated low down.
− bucket and sponge or cloths.
− soap and hand-drying facilities.

Is there adequate space for storing wet paintings and models? Clothes lines and pegs will store paintings temporarily. It is possible to improvise lightweight wooden covers for sand and water trays to give further emergency drying areas. Fablon covering would make cleaning up drips easier. (Remember not to cover wet sand for any length of time.)

Are aprons easy to reach and put away? Keep aprons for water play beside the trolley, and separate from those used for painting. Cotton aprons for cookery activities should be kept with the rest of the cooking equipment.

Ensure that the children can find their own drawing and writing books, and that there is a place for storage when work is finished. Pencils and crayons should be easily accessible and ready for use.

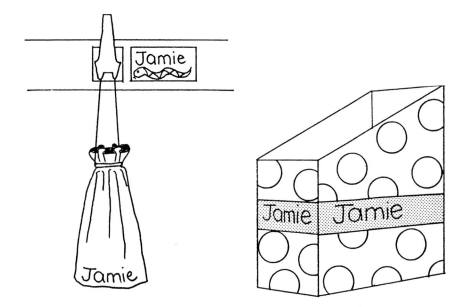

Is there somewhere for children to store their own possessions? Depending on space available, this could be a lidded box on a shelf under the table, a covered soap-powder box stored on a shelving unit, or even a drawstring bag hung from a cup hook.

Division of the classroom

Reading and Listening

This is normally a carpeted area with cushions and easy chairs. It is helpful to have this quiet area screened in some way, by bookcases or other furniture, to add to the privacy and calmness.

As well as in commercially produced bookcases, books can be stored in plastic baskets, or painted soap powder boxes which could be categorised according to subject, and which allow the children to carry books to their desks easily.

Ensure that there is a wide variety of types of books: poetry, reference, pop-up, plays, picture etc. and that the selection is changed regularly – don't forget magazines and newspapers, carefully selected. A display of books related to the topic, or a specific kind of book, e.g. pop-up, could be included, allowing for space available. Book stands made by the children could be used for this – see Library topic. Clear plastic stands made for cookery books also provide useful display stands.

Puppets and dolls are a valuable addition to the reading area. An easy way to store them is to hang them on paint brushes supported in a large tin filled with sand.

Tapes of stories, both commercially produced and made by the children or parents' are popular; also poems, songs and nursery rhymes, together with the written form, and tapes of 'sound effect' stories and music tapes. A junction box enables several children to listen at once with one child responsible for volume control etc. The Language Master machine could also be used here.

A noticeboard at child level, or an easel, could be used for notices relevant to the children e.g. 'Happy Birthday Nupam!' and also for displaying work related to a 'Book of the Week' e.g. reviews, drawings etc.

Clipboards could be available for the children to interview each other, or other adults.

Don't restrict the telephones to the IPA area. Use them in the r.s.l. area to encourage creative speaking. Play the telephone game: provide two telephones. Children sit in a circle and pass one telephone while teacher dials on the other. When teacher 'rings', the child holding the telephone lifts the receiver and speaks to the teacher.

Writing

If practical, this could be situated next to the r.s.l. corner. There should be readily available a supply of various papers, pens, pencils, colouring materials, a typewriter, rulers, rubbers, scissors, glue and adhesive tape, folders, paper clips and fasteners, line guides, handwriting sheets, tracing pictures, blank books, clipboards and dictionaries. Stimulating pictures and photographs could be displayed, plus samples of the children's and adults' writing in different formats e.g. letters, invitations, lists etc. A story chart could provide inspiration. (See Library section.) A home-made 'Word Machine' book can act as a simple thesaurus.

Word resources increase independence and can take many forms. The children's own drawings can be photocopied and labelled, together with the standard word card pockets arranged alphabetically and also in types of words.

Maths

Readily available should be all the basic mathematical equipment for everyday activities, stored logically and clearly labelled. The display would centre around the current topic, with related books, equipment and artefacts. It should be a working display with specific tasks and activities. These tasks should be changed frequently and show a progression of skills e.g. ordering two parcels by weight, progressing to three etc. This area would then provide a ready-made maths activity for the class during an integrated day.

There should be a vocabulary bank of words related to the current topic, either displayed on a board or stored in a box.

Science

As with the Maths area, the display should be a working display related to the current topic. Also, there should be a supply of basic equipment: mirrors, magnifying glasses, Magnispector etc. – depending on school resources and policy.

Art

If space allows, this should be a permanent feature of the classroom, with a plastic-coated cloth over the table. This can be scrubbed by the children in the playground once a week! There should be a wide variety of brushes available, from fine detail brushes to decorating brushes and rollers. As with other areas, it is worth taking the time to train the children to be independent in this area i.e. mix their own paint, pour out glue, and maintain the equipment and materials carefully – storage should allow for and encourage this. Large boxes of powder paint or bottles of glue can be decanted into more manageable sized containers for the children to help themselves.

It is helpful to sort re-useable containers into shapes, (cubes, cylinders etc.) and store in boxes or hanging nets (from the greengrocers). Cereal boxes can be flattened and stored upright.

Sand and water

Equipment for sand and water should be kept separately from the tray. Vegetable storage racks are useful for this. Depending on space, they could be colour coded to facilitate storage, and categorised e.g. standard and non-standard measures. Aprons and cleaning-up materials should be available for the children. Activities should range from free play and investigation to the carrying out of specific tasks written on plastic-covered cards: sand could be wet or dry, and water could be plain, coloured or soapy.

Imaginative play area (IPA)

The theme of this area should be changed frequently, and be more than a 'home corner'. It could reflect the current topic or develop as a result of an event, e.g. a child going on holiday by plane could turn the IPA into an aircraft or travel agency. 'Pretend' windows could be painted and pinned on the walls showing a relevant view.

Appropriate, non-sexist dressing-up clothes should be available. With regard to storage, the clothes can be hung on cup hooks (by a loop sewn on); folded over a curtain wire stretched between two hooks against the wall; draped over a folding clothes horse; folded into an old suitcase, trunk or hamper; or hung from hangers on a mobile clothes rail.

Early days

Try to arrange the room attractively. As there will be no children's creative work available, use commercially produced posters and pictures – perhaps alphabet and number friezes which the children may have met before, or even brightly coloured wrapping paper to cover pin board space. Plants and flowers help to make the room welcoming. Make sure that the various working areas are well organised and that toys, books and equipment are ready and in good condition.

Have a name card ready for each child: first name on one side and both first name and surname on the reverse. Names are special to each of us and children enjoy finding and recognising their own. A motif on the corner of a peelable label each time a child's name occurs will help him/her remember:–

Later, when the child recognises his/her name, the motif could be removed.
Here are some suggestions for motifs, all easy to draw. Use four different colours – giving forty possibilities.

Another idea is to have small name cards, stored in a flat box, each name card with a small piece of Velcro attached to the back. Children find their own name and transfer it to a felt board as they arrive in the room each morning. This can be used later as a counting aid.

There should be named places for coats and shoe bags and, if the cloakroom is some way from the classroom, provide a communal box for cardigans and jerseys.

It is useful to have boxes for home reading folders – an 'in' box next to the teacher's base and an 'out' box next to the door, both clearly marked. It is sensible to have book issuing days and parents should understand fully the organisational procedure the teacher has adopted.

Plastic boxes or trays may be necessary for drinks and packed lunches.

Storage

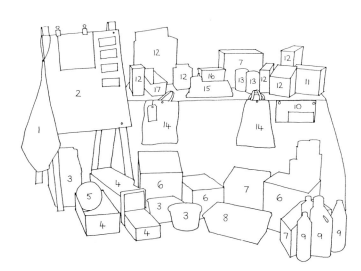

1. Vegetable nets from greeengrocers.
2. Easel – painted and felt-covered; pictures attached with bulldog clips or Velcro strips; cup hooks screwed into frame.
3. Commercially produced plastic boxes.
4. Small boxes covered with wrapping paper.
5. Margarine tub labelled with spirit based pen.
6. Boxes with dividers, e.g. wine bottle boxes, covered with wallpaper.
7. Soap box with cut sides, covered with wrapping paper.
8. Plastic toolbox container; staples etc. in labelled tubs.
9. Commercially produced plastic containers for capacity work.
10. Clear plastic envelopes (e.g. empty felt-tip packs).
11. Miniature drawer units (from DIY shops) for Breakthrough words, split pins etc.
12. Gloss-painted cereal boxes.
13. Tins covered with adhesive plastic.
14. Fruit nets from supermarket for storing small items.
15. Tray for each group of children – containers covered with same wrapping paper for identification purposes.
16. Plastic container for decorator's brushes from DIY shops.
17. Plastic cutlery drainer.

Houses

Stimulus

The song 'How many people live in your house?'

Take a walk to look at houses surrounding school. This probably means going no further than the playground, or it could involve a trip further afield (see section on Outings). Emphasise the danger of building sites. If possible ask a local builder for advice.

Traditional poems: 'The House that Jack Built', 'There was an old woman'.

LANGUAGE

Collections

Books about houses, e.g. *I don't want to live in a house, The Village of Round and Square Houses*.

Large picture of house with room for labelling.

Chart of words in the song 'How many people'.

Lists or individual cards of words beginning with 'h'.

A word resource bank.

Discussion

What is your address?

Where do people live? Talk about different types of housing and homes.

Using large picture of house, label windows, roof, door, gutters etc.

House begins with 'h' . . . can you think of other words beginning with 'h'?

Activities

Using the chart of the words in the song 'How many people?', match individual words written on separate cards to those on the chart.

Write about own homes and families.

Work sheet for sound 'h'.

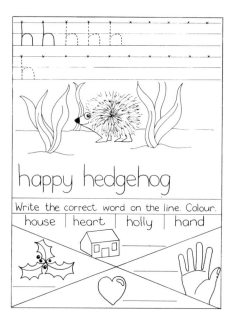

Practise writing letter 'h'.

Make individual books in the shape of a house. Use a page for each room, and draw/write about it.

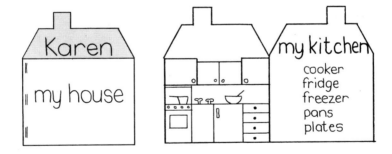

Record own addresses – children could address an envelope for a letter to their parents (perhaps for an invitation or reminder).

Write 'Through my window' stories (see Art and Craft).

Through my window I can see_____.
Through my window I can see_____.
Through my window I can see_____.

MATHEMATICS

Collections

A number line using door shapes – even numbers in one colour, odd in another.

House chart made from shapes.

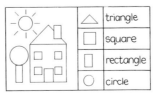

A photograph or drawing of a line of terraced houses. This could be used as a number line.

Discussion

Talk about house numbering, odd and even numbers. Look at houses, see how many shapes are represented; talk about flat shapes and solid shapes.

Look at silhouettes. Be careful to explain new vocabulary adequately: skyline, chimneys, horizon, etc.

Count the windows/doors/chimneys etc. in the line of houses – how are the windows arranged? etc.

Activities

Colour a row of doors, and number them.

Simple worksheet – 'Which door comes before number 9?'

'Which door comes between 3 and 5?'

'Missing set' worksheets, e.g.

Addition bonds.

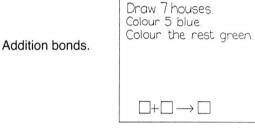

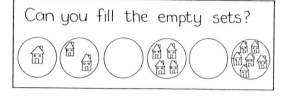

Extend this idea, depending on the children's ability.

Addition bond houses.

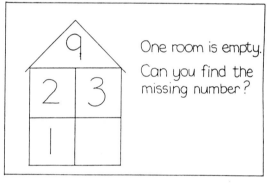

Sort pictures of household items cut from catalogues and glue on to rooms in a house outline.

Worksheet based on the line of houses. How many windows? How many doors?

Use counters or cubes to discover missing numbers.

Make a house of shapes, using adhesive-backed paper.

Shape worksheets.

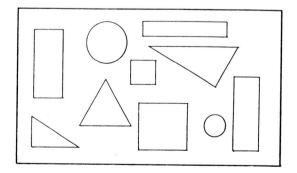

Use bricks such as Poleidoblocs to build 3.D houses.

Graph – How many people live in your house?

What colour is your front door?

(This could be done as a clipboard survey.)

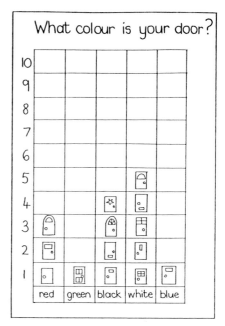

What colour is your door?					
Name	red	green	white	black	blue
Jade			✓		
Peter				✓	

SCIENCE

Collections

Construction toys such as Lego.

House bricks, tiles etc. – materials used to build houses.

Trowels, mallets etc. – builders' tools. Try to borrow a builder's helmet.

Pictures from magazines of different types of houses: terraced, detached, chalet, bungalow etc. (perhaps from different cultures).

Discussion

Talk about different types of houses, using magazine photographs to illustrate points.

Why are some kinds of houses more suitable for old people, and people with babies? Why do we sometimes build flats rather than houses?

Take a walk to look at brick walls – how are the bricks arranged in the wall? What holds them together?

Activities

Make a house using Lego, or similar, to specific instruction (e.g. number of rooms).

Build a wall using house bricks. (Involve a builder if using real bricks.) Perhaps make a raised flower bed. Following this, build a wall, using tissue boxes, arranging them as in the real wall.

Handle and use building trade tools (under close supervision).

Using cardboard cartons, make a house with windows and doors that open. Make cardboard cylinder people to arrange around the house (see photograph p. 17).

ART AND CRAFT

Make a silhouette frieze (see photograph p. 19).

Make 'Through the window' pictures and insert writing (see Language).

Paint a picture of your own house – what colour is your front door and what is its number?

Junk models of houses – individual pictures using techniques used in large display. Make models of own families.

Practise 'ragging' technique using different colour combinations.

Make a 'friendship wall' (making sure each member of the class is included).

MUSIC, MOVEMENT AND IMAGINATIVE PLAY

Songs 'How many people?', 'I have a little tiny house', 'I've just moved into a new house'.

Finger rhymes – a good collection can be found in *This Little Puffin*.

Traditional game 'Round and round the village' from *This Little Puffin*.

Devise a 'building site' mime sequence – include strong movements: cement mixers, building walls etc.

ASSEMBLY

Display in hall: builders' tools, cardboard box wall, junk box house and cylinder people, and pictures of houses.

Begin with the traditional game, 'Round and round the village', *This Little Puffin*.

Talk about builders' work and the tools – individual children could show trowel, helmet etc.

Finish by singing the song 'How many people', illustrating with cylinder people, each one introduced by a different child as it is mentioned in the words of the song.

Books and Stories

I don't want to live in a house by Ann Jungmann and Anni Axworthy, Picture Knight.

Goodbye House by Frank Asch, Picture Corgi.

The Village of Round and Square Houses by Ann Grifalconi, Macmillan.

Poems and Rhymes

Young Puffin Book of Verse has a section entitled 'I will build you a house'.

'Here is a house', 'My little house', 'This is my little house', all in *This Little Puffin*, Puffin Books.

'The house that Jack built', Trad.

'The old woman who lived in a shoe', Trad.

'There was a crooked man', Trad.

Songs and Music

'I've just moved into a new house' in *Tinderbox*, A & C Black.

'How many people live in your house?' in *Tinderbox*, A & C Black.

'All alone in the house' in *Tinderbox*, A & C Black.

'I have a little tiny house' in *Music box Songbook*, BBC.

Nursery Rhymes

Stimulus
Nursery rhymes, recited and sung. This topic concentrates on 'Hickory Dickory Dock' and 'Jack and Jill'. Others can be used similarly.

LANGUAGE

Collections
Books of nursery rhymes.
Nursery rhyme charts.
Sentence cards.
Pictures of clocks.
Word resource bank.

Discussion
Say and sing nursery rhymes.
Can you recognise the rhythm of a nursery rhyme when it is tapped? Play a guessing game.
What sort of clock is in Hickory Dickory Dock? Can you think of other sorts?
Think of rhyming words.
Find variations on nursery rhymes.
How did Jack go down the hill? Think of different words – tumble, roll, crash, bump etc.
How do you go? Think of different ways of moving along. Play a game where one child moves in a particular way, and the others guess.

Activities
Play games using individual words and sentence cards.
Make individual books of favourite nursery rhymes, illustrated by children. Duplicated copies of rhymes could be used.
Rhyming words – make class chart of word families.

Reassemble nursery rhymes
cut into individual lines.

The mouse ran up the clock,

The clock struck one,

The mouse ran down,

Hickory, dickory, c

Hickory, dickory, dock.

1 2 3 4 5 6 7 8 9 10 11 12

Materials: lining paper; 10cm paint brushes; sponges; powder paint in different shades (made up); corrugated cardboard; brown wrapping paper; foil paper; circular shape for clockface; hands and butterfly paperclip; socks; pipe cleaners; cardboard for mouse's head.

Prepare background. Paint lining paper; sponge over contrasting colour.

Make mice. Stuff sock – tie opening securely. Paint circle of card and pipe cleaners pink, twist circle into cone; attach ears with stapler; paint on eyes and nose.

Insert pipe cleaner whiskers. Glue firmly to stuffed sock; attach legs and tail.

Make clockface and clockcase from corrugated card etc. (as shown in photograph). Assemble picture, add captions.

Border: children cut circles of coloured paper, cut into semi-circles and attach to corrugated card strip.

Wall picture – 'How do you go?' (see photograph p. 23).

Work sheets of favourite nursery rhymes – insert the missing words in the gaps.

Zig-zag books of a nursery rhyme (see photograph of wall story).

MATHEMATICS

Collections

Number line based on a counting nursery rhyme.

Pat-a-cake

Pat-a-cake, Pat-a-cake
Baker's ___,
Bake me a ____ as fast as you can.
Pat it and prick it and mark it with 'b',
Put it in the ____
For ____ and me.

draw baby and me.

Once I caught a fish alive

Then I let him go again!

Clocks of various kinds – include timers.

Circles and semicircles – some on paper which can be cut across the centre.

Containers for measurement of capacity activities and chart of useful words (cover with waterproof film if to be used near water trolley – workcards could be similarly covered).

Discussion

Introduce useful vocabulary.

Discuss time sequence through the day, the week, the year. Why do we need clocks?

A clock is usually circular in shape: can you find other circles? What happens when a circle is cut across the middle? What is the new shape called? Introduce words 'whole' and 'half'.

Using containers at water trolley, discuss full, half-full, overflowing, etc.

Activities

Make a class chart of events during the day to show progression of time.

Use a timer to measure various activities and record these in a simple way.

I wrote my name __ times.
I threaded __ beads.
I posted __ bricks into a box.
I skipped __ times.

Provide worksheets using counting nursery rhymes.

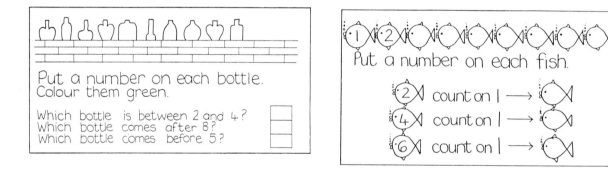

Put a number on each bottle.
Colour them green.

Which bottle is between 2 and 4?
Which bottle comes after 8?
Which bottle comes before 5?

Put a number on each fish.

2 count on 1 ⟶
4 count on 1 ⟶
6 count on 1 ⟶

Sand and water activities involving conservation of quantity – give instruction cards to guide children.

SCIENCE

Visit a park so that children can use swings to experience pendulum action.

Collections

Old clock to take apart.

Pictures of clocks with pendulums.

Cotton reels, weights, buttons, string, plastic bottles.

Vinegar and brown paper.

Objects to investigate rolling and sliding.

Discussion

What happened when we went on the swings?

What is a pendulum? Use pictures of clocks to illustrate.

What happens when we hang a cotton reel from a piece of string and push it?

Discuss what is meant by rolling and sliding.

Activities

Set up a pendulum experiment corner.

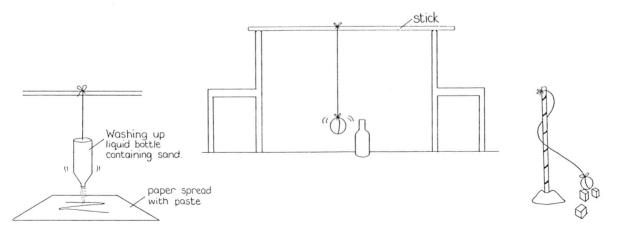

Skittles made of matchboxes or corks – arrange in triangular pattern. Make sure pendulum reaches all skittles.

Set up a rolling/sliding experiment corner.

Investigate slopes. Which shapes roll? Which shapes slide?

What would *we* use for an injury, instead of vinegar and brown paper?

ART AND CRAFT

Using paint and collage technique, make pictures of nursery rhyme characters. Display in a frieze.

Use socks or tights to make other kinds of stuffed toy animals.

Make prints with objects that roll, e.g. cotton reels.

Using the sand pendulum technique (see Science Activities) make pictures using coloured sand.

MUSIC, MOVEMENT AND IMAGINATIVE PLAY

Guess nursery rhyme from rhythm tapped or clapped.

Act out nursery rhymes to a record or tape.

Use percussion instruments to accompany nursery rhymes.

ASSEMBLY

Display in hall: children's collage pictures of nursery rhyme characters.

Begin by acting out a simple nursery rhyme such as 'Jack and Jill' or 'Humpty Dumpty'.

Play the nursery rhyme clapping game, asking children in the audience if they can recognise the rhyme.

Sing several nursery rhymes, perhaps asking for suggestions from the school. Accompany with percussion instruments.

Books and Stories

Each Peach Pear Plum by Janet and Allan Ahlberg, Picture Puffin.

The little dog laughed, illus. by Lucy Cousins, Macmillan.

Nursery Rhymes illus. by Sandy Nightingale, Medici Books.

Puffin Book of Nursery Rhymes, Iona and Peter Opie.

Getting Dressed

Materials: Lining paper; 10cm paint brushes; paint rollers; thin white wash of powder paint; blue/turquoise powder paint (dry); fabric for collage; glue; backing paper; set of paints.

Prepare background: paint strips of lining paper white, sprinkle with dry blue/turquoise paint, roller over to spread dry paint.

Draw around a child to give shape for bear, fill in with fabric scraps.

Draw clothing, fill in with fabric scraps.

Paint bear in shirt, pants, cap and shoes.

Border of shirts in pattern that teacher starts.

Stimulus

Read the story 'How do I put it on?' by Shigeo Watanabe, Picture Puffin.

LANGUAGE

Collections

Books about bears.

Children's own teddy bears.

Scraps of fur, velvet – fabrics that have a soft, furry texture in 'feeling' box or bag.

A selection of hats – real or home-made, e.g. top hat, clown's hat, bonnet etc.

Lists on individual cards of words beginning with 'b'.

Word resource bank.

Discussion

What is the sensible order for putting on garments in the morning or after P.E.? Why do we put shoes on last?

Can you peg clothes on a washing line in order?

Which words describe teddy bears (furry, soft, warm etc.)?

Can you hear the 'b' sound at the beginning of 'bear'?

Play the 'clothes game' – 'If you're wearing blue, take a step forward/go and line up etc.'

Activities

Write about your teddy bear.

Make individual friezes about getting dressed. Label clothes using ordinal number words – first, second, third etc.

Make a class story book about a little bear and his adventures.

Think of a good name for the bear.

Work sheets for sound 'b'. Practise writing letter 'b'.

Dressing bear game.

Use hats to stimulate oral and written work – 'When I put on the clown's hat I feel . . .'

Draw a picture of you in your favourite outfit, and write a sentence.

MATHEMATICS

Collections

A number line using shirt or teddy bear outline.

A set of cards.

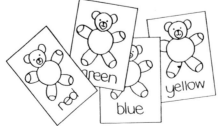

four red, four blue
four green, four yellow.

A set of cards for number language – 'smaller', 'bigger'.

A set of cards with pictures of clothes, some adults', some children's, cut from magazines.

Circles for Venn diagrams (either hoops or drawn).

The following phrases appear within the photograph:

first   second   third   fourth

I put on my vest and my pants.

I put on my skirt or my trousers and my jumper.

I put on my socks or my tights.

Last of all I put on my shoes.

Discussion

Introduce ordinal numbers. Using bear cards in stand, ask questions e.g. 'What colour is the third bear' etc?

Can you arrange the teddy bear collection in order of size? Talk about patterns.

Can you sort the clothes cards a) according to who wears them b) types of clothes (coat etc)?

Activities

Make patterns with a variety of equipment, e.g. beads, Unifix, buttons.

Colour stripes on shirts – finish the pattern.

Repeat pattern of cut-out clothes (e.g. shirts as in border of photograph page 00).

Make a chart of children's teddy bears in order of size. Label appropriately e.g. 'Karen's bear is the smallest', 'Tim's bear is the fourth in the line' etc.

Addition bonds.

Colour 2 bears blue.
Colour 3 bears red.

$2 + 3 \rightarrow$

Ordinal number work sheets.

Number the bears.

Colour the first bear red.
Colour the second bear blue.
Colour the third bear green.
Colour the fourth bear yellow.
Colour the fifth bear orange.

How do you get dressed?

1st   2nd   3rd   4th   5th   6th

SCIENCE

Collections

Children's own teddy bears.

Fabric scraps.

Boxes, paper clips, glue etc. for model making.

Fasteners of various kinds.

Lego or construction toys.

Discussion

Why do animals have fur?

Talk about different kinds of body covering.

How do animals keep their fur clean?

Activities

Experiment with hot water bottle to demonstrate insulation qualities of fur.

Make a model of bear using butterfly paper fasteners to join cardboard head, body, arms etc., so that joints move.

'Fastenings' table, where children can experiment using different materials.

Make a house for the three bears using construction toys: put in it beds, chairs and so on.

Make a wardrobe with doors that open for the bears' clothes.

ART AND CRAFT

Make group frieze of sequence of dressing (see photograph page 27).

Draw round own teddy bear to give outline, then mix paint to match colour. Cut out and mount for wall display, with children's descriptive sentence beneath.

Use plastic modelling material to make 3D teddybears.

Make an individual picture of yourself wearing clothes for a particular occasion, e.g. swimming, using collage technique.

Make 'dress-a-person' game. Trace over outline of a person to make clothes for him/her. Attach with temporary fixative, e.g. Blu-Tack.

DRAMA AND IMAGINATIVE PLAY

Act out the story of Goldilocks and the Three Bears.

Arrange IPA as the three bears' house. Make head-dresses for the three bears, labels etc.

ASSEMBLY

Display in the hall: washing line, basket of clothes and container of pegs.

Begin by discussing getting dressed – ask individual children from the onlookers to help by pegging clothes on the line in the correct/sensible order.

Have own class sitting in four groups – 1) all have shirts, 2) all have pants, 3) all have caps, 4) all have a pair of shoes.

Teacher tells story – the groups act out what happens.

Finish by singing 'The Three Bears', *Okki Tokki Unga*.

Books and Stories

Little Bear books by Shigeo Watanabe, Picture Puffin.

Mr Bear books by Chizuko Kuratomi, Macdonald.

Can't you sleep, little bear? by Martin Waddell and Barbara Firth, Walker Books.

Old Bear by Jane Hussey, Beaver Books.

Little Bear's Trousers by Jane Hussey, Beaver Books.

Tom and Pippo and the Washing Machine by Helen Oxenburg, Walker Books.

Mrs Mopple's Washing Line by Anita Hewett, Puffin.

Poems and Rhymes

'Teddy Bear' by Aileen Fisher in *Young Puffin Book of Verse*.

Songs and Music

'The Three Bears' in *Okki Tokki Unga*, A & C Black.

'Round the Mulberry Bush' (using clothes), Trad.

Jack and the Beanstalk

Word resource bank.

Stimulus

Read the story of Jack and the Beanstalk.

Sing the song 'We are going to plant a bean'.

Plant beans. (Remember packeted beans for gardeners are very often treated with fungicide.)

LANGUAGE

Collections

Different versions of the traditional story.

Beans of various kinds (haricot, aduki, kidney etc).

Discussion

Is the story real or make believe? How can you tell?

Was Jack sensible to exchange the cow for the beans?

Why was his mother cross?

If you grew a magic beanstalk, what would you like to find at the top of it?

Examine and compare the beans.

Find other words that mean 'big' and 'small'.

Activities

Draw a magic beanstalk and what you would like to find at the top of it.

Tell the story in pictures with captions – possibly a zig-zag book for each child.
Missing word sentences (work sheet).

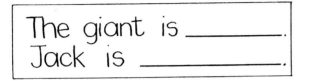

The giant is _____.
Jack is _____.

A whale is _____ than a goldfish.
A mouse is _____ than an elephant.

Draw the giant and write about him. What does he say?

MATHEMATICS

Collections

Leaf number line – use two shades of green, one for odd, one for even numbers. Make 10, 20 etc. as flowers. (See photograph, page 25.)
Cards of useful mathematical words; big, small, long, tall etc.
Beans – a variety of sizes.
Leaves of different sizes and squared paper/Unifix bricks.

Discussion

Use and explain words of comparison: bigger, smaller, taller, etc. Relate to leaves.
Introduce signs > (more than) < (less than) – e.g. 5>2, 3<6.
Talk about odd and even numbers. Count in twos.
Play games estimating how many beans in a group.

Activities

Find the number of squares a leaf covers using squared paper or Unifix bricks – compare different sizes of leaves.
Arrange beans in order of size – glue to a card.
How many beans in a group?

this boat is bigger than this boat

this flower is smaller than this flower

this giraffe is bigger than the giraffe

the giant is bigger than Jack

Jack is smaller than the giant

this shark is smaller than this shark

Make collage pictures of things to illustrate 'bigger than: smaller than'
Count in twos – make a list of things which come in twos.

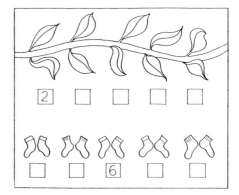

SCIENCE

Collections

Beans, separately and in pods.
Leaves of different kinds.
Pots, jars, compost etc. for planting beans.
Prepared food containing beans.

Discussion

What are the beans like? Talk about size, colour, shape.
What is a bean? What happens to it when it is planted? What are the leaves like?
Discuss the life cycle of a plant.
What do we eat which is made from beans?

Activities

Plant various kinds of beans using different methods:–

– In jam jars lined with blotting paper – stuff the centre with cotton wool, tissues or sand to prevent beans from falling to the bottom. Surround jar with a tube of black paper to speed germination.
– In peat pots in compost.
– On damp cotton wool.

Try the above with cooked beans.

Keep careful records of all growing experiments – a written diary, either individual or group.
Make a graph of the rate of growth.

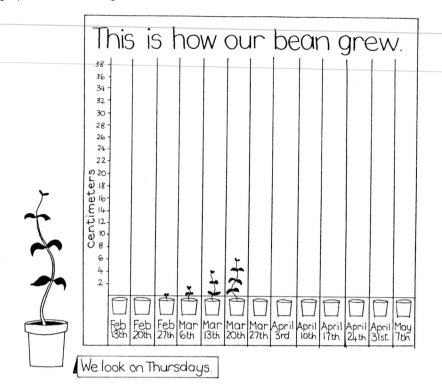

This activity will stimulate discussion during the growing process – introduce appropriate vocabulary as the need arises (roots, stems, leaves, shoots etc.).

Weigh, soak and re-weigh dried butter beans. What change do you observe? Cut or break open a soaked bean. What is inside?

Taste products made with beans.

ART AND CRAFT

Print with leaves – paint reverse side of many leaves, lay on chosen background, cover with a sheet of newspaper and roller over. Remove leaves carefully, trying not to smudge.

'Magic trees' from rolled newspapers. Tightly roll newspaper diagonally and glue final corner. Fringe the top, then gently pull out from the centre.

Make bean and seed collage pictures/patterns.

DRAMA

Explore aspects of growing and shrinking.

ASSEMBLY

Display in hall: bean plants, leaf print pictures, collage bean and seed pictures.

Begin by showing the onlookers the bean plants and the beans from which they grew.

Sing the song 'We are going to plant a bean' (*This Little Puffin*).

Act out the story of Jack, using percussion instruments to accompany the action. Make a beanstalk with 'magic tree' technique to 'grow' at the appropriate moment.

Books and Stories

Jim and the Beanstalk by Raymond Briggs, Picture Puffin.
Jack and the Beanstalk by Fran Hunia in Read it Yourself series, Ladybird.
Hairy Tales and Nursery Crimes by Michael Rosen, Young Lions, Armada Books.

Poems and Rhymes

'A spike of green' by Barbara Fisher in *Young Puffin Book of Verse*.

Songs and Music

'We are going to plant a bean' in *This Little Puffin* compiled by Elizabeth Matterson, Puffin.

Packed Lunches

Materials: Lining paper; paint rollers; spray bottles; blue/turquoise/white paints; silver poster paint; fruit nets from supermarket fruit packs; tissue paper; waste products to make 3D models.

Prepare background – paint blue/turquoise (different shades for sky and sea). When dry, spray sea with white paint to create froth effect.

Make boats, rocks, cottage, lighthouse using paint/collage/waste materials.

Make picnic basket – use wax rubbing over woven straw mat. Cut out net shape of basket, fold and glue.

Make seagulls from white paper, white tissue feathers and gold foil beaks.

Border: blue strip cut to make wave shape, paint underwater scene using silver, pink and green paints.

Stimulus
Organise an outing involving the need for a packed lunch, or have packed lunches together in school.
Read the stories *The Lighthouse Keeper's Lunch* and *The Giant Jam Sandwich*.

LANGUAGE
Collections
Equipment for a picnic: basket, lunch box, flask etc.
Pictures of people having picnics.
Magazines from which to cut pictures.
Word resource banks.

Discussion
What do you like in your packed lunch? How do you make a sandwich?
What sort of fillings can be used?
How do you eat a packed lunch?
Can you think of good items to include in a packed lunch in summertime/wintertime, or for a specific situation, such as a climbing trip or a seaside outing?
What kinds of food could be included?

The lighthouse keeper's wife made horrible mustard sandwiches – can you think of others? Which words describe them (disgusting, nasty, revolting etc.)? Can you think of delicious sandwiches? Which words describe them?

Where do people go for picnics? Different outings/trips.

Activities

Re-tell the story of 'The Lighthouse Keeper' in own words, using the teacher as the scribe. Can you change the story?

Make picnic menus – try to include all sorts of food.

Record pictorially.

> This is what we took to eat for our packed lunch.
> pitta bread and cheese
> a tomato
> orange
> crisps
> a drink
> crack!
> a biscuit
> a banana
> Yum yum!

Draw and write about delicious/disgusting sandwiches

Make individual picnic books.

> Where shall we have our picnic? — front cover
> We could picnic in our garden. — first page
> or we could go to the seaside — inside pages
> or we could stay at home if it is raining! — back page

Make scrapbooks using magazines for pictures of food in a picnic hamper – a group of children could compile this together. Design a checked picnic cloth for the cover and decide, as a group, where the picnic will take place and title the book accordingly, e.g. 'Blue Group's Seaside Picnic, by John, Sara and Claire'.

Complete hidden word squares e.g. things to put in sandwiches.

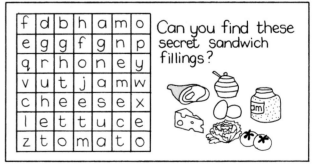

f	d	b	h	a	m	o
e	g	g	f	g	n	p
q	r	h	o	n	e	y
v	u	t	j	a	m	w
c	h	e	e	s	e	x
l	e	t	t	u	c	e
z	t	o	m	a	t	o

Can you find these secret sandwich fillings?

MATHEMATICS

Collection

Articles with checked patterns – tablecloths, teatowels,

game boards etc.

Cubes, Unifix and Multilink.

All sizes of squared paper.

Pegboards.

Cardboard boxes of different shapes and sizes.

Commercial games involving squared boards and dice, e.g. snakes and ladders.

Equipment and ingredients for breadmaking.

Coinage in 1p, 2p, 5p and 10p.

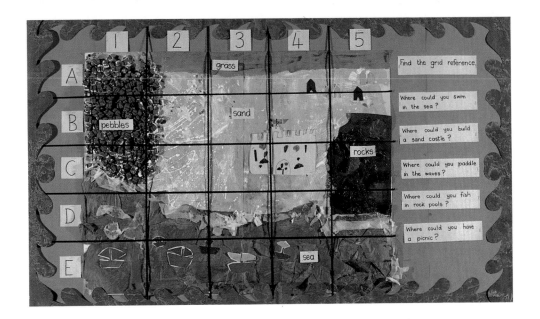

Discussion

Compare the articles with squared patterns – talk about similarities and differences – size of squares, number of squares etc.

How can you arrange the squares to change the pattern?

Talk about squares – how many corners? How many sides? What do you notice about the sides?

Explain simple grids (numbered squares used in map reference).

Talk about and demonstrate how to play games based on a chequerboard.

Activities

Make 'picnic cloths' from squared paper, either by gluing or colouring squares.

Experiment with repeating patterns.

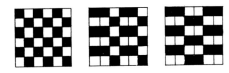

Make bread (see Science Activities). Use the loaves to make sandwiches.

Following sandwich-making activities, use adhesive squares to find out in how many ways a sandwich can be cut (Tangrams).

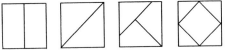

Investigate cutting slices in different directions from loaves of different shapes (cottage, bloomer etc.).

Calculate how many different sandwiches you can make using two/three/four fillings.

Price the sandwiches and devise buying and selling activities (see Drama and IPA).

Use peg boards and Unifix cubes to create squared and symmetrical patterns. Transfer to squared paper.

Practise 'packing' sandwiches into lunch box. Can you fit them in to use the available space to maximum effect? Use this activity to lead on to packing recyclable materials (cubes and cuboids) into a larger box.

Play and devise simple board games using chequerboards and dice (this could be tackled by a small group of children working in co-operation).

Make a 'seaside' or 'countryside' picture to use as the basis of map reference activities (see photograph).

Investigate pentominoes.

Play noughts and crosses.

SCIENCE

Collections

Equipment and ingredients for breadmaking.

Materials for making picnic container, wrapping sandwiches, building a lighthouse etc.

Equipment to make a simple electrical circuit (for a lighthouse lamp).

Discussion

Talk about carrying a packed lunch and wrapping the food – what makes the most suitable wrapping (Clingfilm, greaseproof paper etc)? How are take-away meals wrapped?

How did the lighthouse keeper's wife send the basket to the lighthouse? How do you suppose she got it back?

The people of Itching Down used helicopters to lift the giant jam sandwich. Can you think of other ways to move a large unwieldy object?

What is the best way to carry a packed lunch?

Activities

Make a picnic container with a carrying handle – devise a test to show how heavy a load it will take.

Make bread for a packed lunch – discuss the process involved as the activity takes place.

Make and wrap sandwiches.

Find ways of transferring the lighthouse keeper's lunch to and from the lighthouse (pulley etc).

Build a lighthouse and make a simple electrical circuit to light up the lamp.

Make a machine to lift the giant jam sandwich.

ART AND CRAFT

Make seascape pictures using paint and collage.

Make a large checked cloth using paper squares. Set out picnic on paper plates – each child makes own favourite picnic food, with collage materials.

Make a frieze of the story of the Giant Jam Sandwich. Two children could co-operate on each section.

Make 'sandwiches' from sponges, and dough biscuits etc. for sandwich bar.

DRAMA AND IMAGINATIVE PLAY

Provide the 'props' needed for a picnic – use IPA as a picnic place.

Set up a sandwich bar for imaginative play – provide a telephone to take orders etc.

ASSEMBLY

Display in hall: big model of lighthouse and a painting of the Grinling's cottage (pinned to hall pinboard) – connect them with a line.

Begin by telling the story of 'The Lighthouse Keeper's Lunch'.

Demonstrate how a pulley works (see Science section).

Describe the work of a lighthouse – why they are needed to protect shipping etc.

Play a tape of 'Fingals Cave', or 'Sea Symphony'.

Books and Stories

The Lighthouse Keeper's Lunch by Ronda and David Armitage, Picture Puffin.

The Giant Jam Sandwich,. story and pictures by John Vernon Lord, verses by Janet Burroway, Pan Books.

My naughty little sister goes fishing by Dorothy Edwards and Shirley Hughes, Little Mammoth.

Poems and Rhymes

'There are big waves' by Eleanor Farjeon in *Young Puffin Book of Verse*.

'Puffin Book of Salt Sea Verse compiled by Charles Causley.

'Bread and Jam' in *This Little Puffin*, compiled by Elizabeth Matterson.

Songs and Music

'Until I saw the sea' in *Tinderbox*, A & C Black.

'When an Elephant's Feeling Hungry' in *Game Songs with Prof. Dogg's Troupe*, A & C Black.

'The Super Supper March, *Appuskidu*, A & C Black.

'Fingal's Cave' by Mendelssohn.

'Sea Symphony' by Vaughan Williams.

Presents

Stimulus

A celebration – Christmas/birthday/Divali etc.

The story of *Mr. Rabbit and the Lovely Present.*

LANGUAGE

Collections

Wrapping paper; parcels of different objects for guessing game – some soft, some that rattle etc; greetings cards – birthday, congratulations etc; pictures of parties, wedding receptions, birthday cakes; decorated box with hinged lid (see Maths, Art and Craft); small objects to put in box – car, ball, doll, boat, ring, cup, toy dog/cat etc.

Feeling box.

Word resource bank.

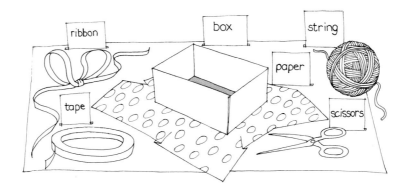

Discussion

When is your birthday?

When and why do we give presents?

Talk about the parcels – describe them – are they hard, soft, do they rattle . . .?

Play a memory game with the lidded box – put objects inside (increase the number as the children become used to the idea); wait a while, then see if the objects can be named. Increase the length of time between initiation and completion of game.

Use 'feeling box' to extend vocabulary.

Activities

Choose a parcel and imagine what is inside. Write about it.

Make cards for specific occasions. Think of appropriate message for inside.

Make a present for a partner; wrap it and 'send' it (see IPA suggestions); then write to thank your friend.

Extend memory game (play in pairs or small group):
–   Write down the names of objects your friend puts in the box.
–   Guess what is in the box – give clues/ask questions, e.g. Does it begin with 'c'? Has it got wheels? etc.

Play a cumulative memory game – 'For my birthday I received a book', 'For my birthday I received a book and a teddy bear' etc.

Make a class book of suitable presents for mother/dog/grandmother etc.

WHAT SHALL WE GIVE THEM?

MATHEMATICS

Collections

Papier mâché fruit (see Art and Craft).

Basket or suitable container for 'fruit'.

Parcels of different shapes, sizes and weights – small/heavy, large/light.

Clipboards.

Commercially produced boxes – chocolate boxes come in an amazing variety of shapes.

Discussion

Using papier mâché fruit and basket, explore estimation and approximation (calculating probabilities) – e.g. Will there be enough for each child to have a piece? Which colour will I pick out? How many pieces must be chosen to have two of the same colour? Investigate.

Talk about different shapes of commercially produced boxes.

What do we have to put on parcels which are to be sent through the post?

Activities

Take different boxes apart to show the plane shapes involved.

Draw around the faces of a box in order to demonstrate its net.

Make 'nets' of chocolate boxes. Which net relates to which box? (See photograph page 39).

Make own boxes using squared paper to plan net (younger children need help here). Do not use 'tabs' – masking tape is good for sealing edges.

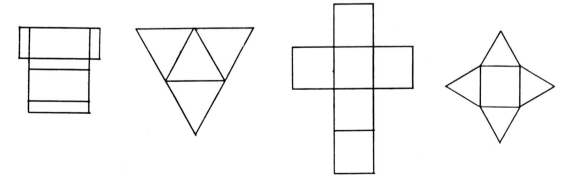

Estimate amount of paper needed to wrap boxes of different sizes.

Balance and weigh parcels – 'Which is heaviest?' etc. The parcels can be identified by colour or number.

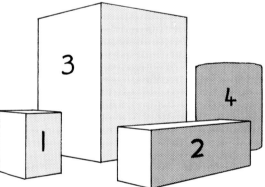

Carry out a clipboard survey to find the most popular fruit – devise a graph to illustrate your findings.

SCIENCE

Collections

Paper of different types and weights.

Packaging – corrugated cardboard, polystyrene chips, egg boxes, cardboard party plates and dishes, shredded paper, masking tape, adhesive tape and glue.

String, wool, twine, cotton thread of different thicknesses and materials.

Discussion

What is used for wrapping parcels which are to be posted?

Discuss merits of various sorts of packaging.

How can we stop fragile items from being broken?

Activities

Using materials provided, devise package to protect an object, such as a box of chalk, from breaking when dropped through the letter box. Devise a fair test to prove the efficiency of your packaging.

Test strengths of different sorts of paper: does it make a difference when the paper is wet?

Wrap up parcels using different sorts of paper and investigate the ways in which the parcel can be secured.

Devise a test to show the strength of various types of string/wool/cotton/twine etc.

Find ways to wrap up different solid shapes – cylinders, cones, cubes etc.

ART AND CRAFT

Make wrapping paper for presents using a variety of techniques e.g. marbling, wax resist.

Decorate your net before making up into a box (see Maths).

Make papier mâché objects such as fruit using a crumpled newspaper base covered with strips of paste-soaked newspaper. To complete the shape, cover with white paper and finally coloured tissue paper or paint. Avoid paste with fungicide.

Free collage work using a wide variety of materials – try restricting each picture to shades and tones of one colour – find as many different textures as possible.

Drawings in paper of primary colour – outline in thick black felt-tip pen, then cut out and mount on different shade of chosen colour (see main photograph).

Design postage stamps to put on parcels.

DRAMA AND IMAGINATIVE PLAY

Make IPA a post office: provide appropriate equipment e.g. stamp pad, paper and envelopes, 'stamps', scales for weighing parcels, money etc.

ASSEMBLY

Display in hall: box 'presents' the class has made in artwork.

Act out the story of *Mr Rabbit and the lovely present*. The main characters are Mr Rabbit (make headdress with long ears) and the little girl.

Divide rest of class into four groups: red, blue, yellow and green. Each child makes a hat of appropriate colour using collage technique. The four groups make four circles sitting cross-legged with apples, pears, bananas and grapes on the floor in the centre. Teacher or a child tells the story, allowing main characters to speak – progressing from group to group collecting the fruit and finally assembling the basket of fruit.

Finish the assembly by talking about giving and receiving gifts and saying 'Thank you'.

Books and Stories
Mr Rabbit and the Lovely Present by Charlotte Zolotow, Picture Puffin.
The Surprise Party by Pat Hutchins, Picture Puffin.

Poems and rhymes
'What is Pink' by Christina Rossetti in *Young Puffin Book of Verse*, Penguin.
'The Hippopotamus's Birthday' by E. V. Rieu in *I like this poem*, edited by Kaye Webb, Puffin.

Songs and Music
'My ship sailed from China', *Appuskidu*, A & C Black.
'The Marvellous Toy' by Tom Paxton in *Ramblin'*, Harmony Music Ltd.
'Bendy Toy' in *Game Songs with Prof. Dogg's Troupe*, A & C Black.

Night and Day

Stimulus

Visit a zoo or bird sanctuary to observe owls.

Watch the progress of the sun through the sky. Do **not** look directly at the sun.

Invite a night-worker e.g. nurse, police officer, to talk about working at night.

Read *The Owl who was afraid of the Dark*.

LANGUAGE

Collections

Pictures and photographs of scenes by day and night.

Pictures and models of owls.

Words to describe various times of the day – dawn, morning, noon etc.

Word resource bank.

Discussion

Which words describe owls?

When do owls hunt, and when and where do they sleep? Not all owls are nocturnal.

Which words describe the day and the night?

In some countries owls are thought to be unlucky – why do you think that people have this idea?
Other people think that they are wise birds. Why?
Some people work whilst we sleep: who, and why?
Talk about the feeling of the owl who was afraid of the dark.

Activities

Describe your day. Using the words you have learnt (dawn, morning etc.) make a diary of a day in your life and illustrate it.
Imagine that you are a nightworker and describe your work. Is it difficult to sleep during the day?
In pairs or small groups write poems about owls/day/night. Present as a calligram.
Make word pictures of owls.

Make a survey of the days in which the children in your class were born – use this information to write a story based on 'Sunday's Child' (Trad).

MATHEMATICS

Collections
Calendars and diaries of different kinds.

Discussion
Describe the sequence of morning, afternoon, evening etc. – extend this to week, month, year.
How are days different in summer and winter (day length)? Talk about the annual cycle.
Which things happen daily, weekly, monthly, yearly?

Activities
Make calendars of different kinds. Devise different ways of recording the date.
Make a birthday chart of the children in your class.

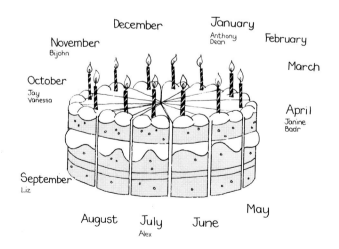

Owl hunts at night.

Words that describe night.

gentle · shadowy · gloomy · peaceful · soft · still · dark · mysterious · velvety · secret · starry · sleepy · quiet · calm

Woodchip wall paper painted appropriate colour with large brushes or rollers. Owl collage using shades of brown and beige cut from magazines. Overlap from bottom to give a 'feathery' appearance. Add stars, tree, moon. Repeat to make daytime picture using appropriate colours.

Make a chart of the things that happen daily, weekly, etc.
Make a chart showing length of time spent awake and asleep.

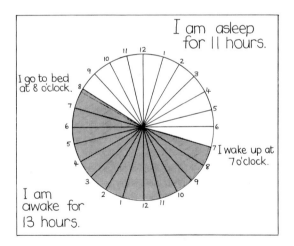

I am asleep for 11 hours.

I go to bed at 8 o'clock.

I wake up at 7 o'clock.

I am awake for 13 hours.

SCIENCE

Collections

Large pictures of owls.
Reference books about owls.
Recordings of owl calls, on tape.
A sterilized owl pellet to examine and analyse.
An owl pellet that has been analysed (try local museum or zoological society).
A terrestrial globe and torch.

Discussion

Talk about the owl: its eyes, ears, feathers, feet.
Listen to the call of the owl.
Discuss its habitat and hunting methods.
Talk about the owl pellet and the bones found in it.
Discuss why owls are in danger. Talk about relationship between predator and prey.

Explain the terms diurnal and nocturnal.

Explain why we have night and day (sun as a light source).

Activities

Examine an owl pellet and categorise the objects found in it.

Using globe and torch experiment – investigate which countries are in daylight and which are in darkness.

Devise a chart to illustrate which animals are diurnal and which are nocturnal.

ART AND CRAFT

Paint with feathers.

Make an owl of thumb/finger prints – which other techniques might be used (pastels, wax resist etc.)?

Day and night pictures – paint an outdoor picture in bright colours (tree/house/snowman) – now repeat the picture, but using 'night' colours: grey, mauve, purple, black.

Make wax scratch night pictures.

Make individual pictures of night workers into a frieze.

MOVEMENT, MUSIC AND IMAGINATIVE PLAY

Tell the story of *Goodnight Owl* using different instruments to represent the creatures in the story.

ASSEMBLY

Display in hall: paintings of owls; frieze of nightworkers.

Play 'Moonlight Sonata'.

Talk about people who work during the night: ask for suggestions from the rest of the school.

Tell the story of *Goodnight Owl*, using different instruments to represent the creatures in the story.

Finish by reciting an 'owl' poem.

Books and Stories

The Owl who was afraid of the Dark by Jill Tomlinson, Puffin.

Goodnight Owl by Pat Hutchins, Puffin.

Owl at home by Arnold Lobel in 'I can read' series, Worlds Work Ltd.

One Moonlit Night by Ronda and David Armitage, Picture Puffin.

Poems and Rhymes

'Owl and the Pussycat' by Edward Lear in *I like this poem*, edited by Kaye Webb, Puffin.

'Moths and Moonshine' by James Reeves in *Young Puffin Book of Verse*, compiled by Barbara Ireson, Puffin.

'The Months' by Christina Rossetti in *I like this poem*, edited by Kaye Webb, Puffin.

'The Owl', in *Puffin Book of Nursery Rhymes*, Iona and Peter Opie.

Songs and Music

'Days of the Month', *Harlequin*, A & C Black.

'Each day different', *Harlequin*, A & C Black.

'Moonlight Sonata' by Beethoven.

Libraries

Stimulus

A visit to the local library.

A talk by a librarian.

A visit by a mobile library.

The setting up or development of a school/classroom library.

LANGUAGE

Collection

Old library cards and tickets.

Leaflets and posters from the local library.

Dust jackets.

Posters advertising specific books.

Colour coded stickers.

Reviews of books from children's magazines/bookclubs.

Collections of different types of books e.g. pop-up, miniature, poetry, other languages.

Different writing implements e.g. quill pen, typewriter, pencil etc.

Braille books.

Discussion

Who is a member of a library?

How do you join?

Does it cost anything?

Why do you join?

Discuss how to use the library; the computerised system; fines; the job of a librarian.

Which/where is the nearest library?

Discuss special provision for the handicapped, e.g. Braille, large print, books on tape.

Activities

Put words in alphabetical order.
Write book reviews.

Keep reading diaries.

Book Review Card I

★ Write the title and author.

★ Write when the book was printed and the name of the publisher.

★ Describe how the story begins. (use your own words)

★ Did you like the beginning? Why?

★ If you did not like it, write a new one.

Read and discuss published reviews.

Name the parts of a book i.e. spine, cover, pages.

Look at the information given in a book: date and name of publisher, dedication etc., introduction, resumé on back, contents and index page, title page, author, illustrator etc.

Investigate different types of writing.

Consider the audience of a book – who is it written for? How can you tell?

Ask parents to write short stories for the classroom library about their child using *My Naughty Little Sister* as a model.

Study and compare works by the same author, e.g. Roald Dahl.

Write stories using the 'consequence' method: each child writes a beginning. These are then redistributed among the class and each child continues the story they were given, and writes a middle. The process is repeated for the endings (see photograph page 47).

Write books individually or in groups, perhaps using a typewriter or word processor.

Write stories with morals, modelled on Aesop.

Send invitations to local authors, illustrators or a publisher, to visit and talk to the children.

Record interviews with members of staff/parents/other classes about favourite authors or stories.

Set up a class library with a 'favourite book' theme, chosen and run by two children every week.

Find out how to use reference books

Practise scanning to find specific information from a book.

Make comparisons between the same story told by different authors.

Write/investigate a simple history of books.

Find out how a book is produced and sold; the role of editor, designer, printer, bookseller, etc.

Discuss ways of indexing books: colour? subject? author? number references?

Set up a writing corner.

Come and Write !

Author's Gallery

lines
tracing
coloured
white
borders
card

Beginning. Middle. End.

Ask the children to draw and colour pictures of themselves, dressed in their favourite clothes. Use the stories written using the 'consequences' method (see Language Activities). Glue each section on to white paper, and cut out in a 'thought bubble' shape. Now cut an identical bubble in black paper and display with the black one dropped down to create the illusion of a shadow. Repeat for small bubbles. Use a potato to print footsteps.

Write in a specific style e.g. Roald Dahl's *BFG*.
Keep a book log to record what children have read. (The children could take charge of this.)
Write a short autobiography to go in the back of home-made books.
Devise story charts.

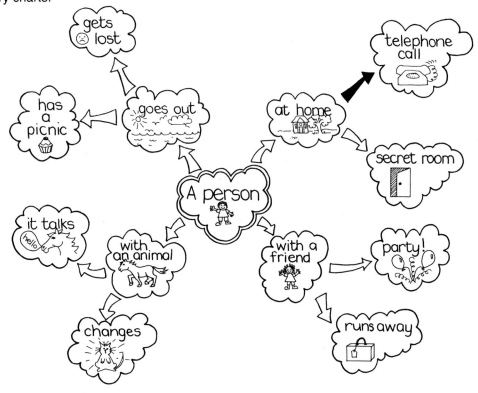

MATHEMATICS

Collection
Circles for Venn diagrams (either hoops or drawn).
Skeleton Carroll diagrams and pathways.

Within the diagram: No · Yes · Yes · No · Is it taller than 30 cm? · Is it taller than 30 cm? · Yes · No · Is it fiction? · Put the books which need sorting here.

Dust jackets to study construction and prices.

Discussion
Talk about the cost of books and compare with other items.
Fines from public libraries – how much are they? Why are we fined?
Look at odd and even page numbers. Are they always on the left or right hand side?
Which page is the *first* page?
Look at page numbering: some books miss out numbers because of illustrations and photographs.

Activities
Make graphs of favourite authors, books, poems.
Categorise books for colour coding using Venn diagrams, Carroll diagrams and pathways.
Measure book dimensions.
Calculate average number of words per line/lines per page to find how many words on a page (use a calculator).
Investigate the occurrence of particular letters to be recorded on a block graph.
Make a map of the route to the public library or school library.
Draw a plan of the library showing where subjects are.
Make dust jackets for a particular book by measuring.
Make individual books; count and predict the number of sides and pages to see the correspondence.
Make zig-zag books: look at the relationship between folds and resulting pages.

SCIENCE

Collection
A wide variety of papers and card.
A wide variety of glues e.g. PVA, water based cellulose glue, flour and water, glue sticks etc.
Book binding tapes, paper fasteners, staples, paper clips, needle and thread.
Transparent adhesive-backed plastic.

Discussion
Examine and compare ways of producing books.
The value of hardbacked covers.
The value of plastic coating.

Activities
Test paper strengths.
Test glue strengths.
Test paper folding rates.
Make paper.
Use stories for technology e.g. design and build a bridge for the Three Billy Goats Gruff.
Using pop-up and peephole books, create new versions with paper fasteners etc.

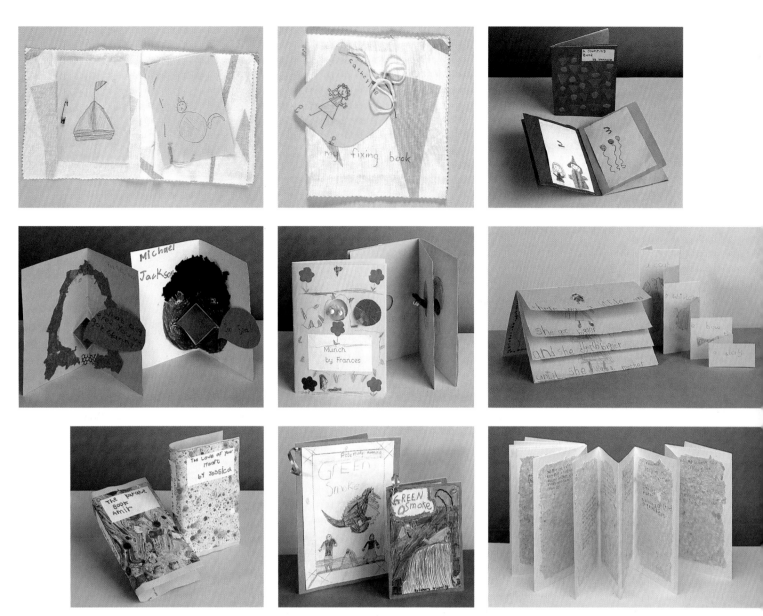

My Fixing Book:
Material pages, sewn up the spine. Pictures/writing done on pieces of paper: each has to be attached to its page using a different technique e.g. glue, string, pin, staple etc.

Counting Book:
Make a simple Maths book, possibly for younger child e.g. nursery, sibling.

Pop-Up Book:
Fold a piece of paper in half. Make a small cut in from folded edge. Open, score 4 creases (illus.). Fold in half again, ensuring the paper folds along the scored lines to form the mouth. Attach another piece of paper to the back, gluing round the edges only. Draw the rest of a face around the mouth.

Munch:
Make a book with a hole in the same place on every page, large enough to put a finger through. Make a caterpillar from felt to fit a child's finger. Glue the body on to the back so that the head can poke through all pages.

Expanding Books:
a) Make a concertina – cut the top to different levels.
b) Using 2 pieces of A4 paper, stagger and fold in two so that you can see four steps. Open out and staple along fold. Close and use. Make a cover if required.

Imitation Book:
Use pieces of polystyrene, glue card on for cover.

Reviews:
Write reviews and reports on books, and make into books, with a redesigned cover.

Handmade-paper Books:
Recycle old paper. Colour a small proportion one colour, and the remainder another. Into each page, insert a small dot of the other coloured pulp. Use this paper to write a story: 'And That's How I Got My Pink Dot!' The stories should be totally ridiculous: use *On the Way Home* by Jill Murphy for inspiration.

ART AND CRAFT

Design dust jackets.

Design posters for book advertisements.

Bind books in various ways, including sewing.

Make marbled paper for book covers.

Make detailed drawings of the children reading their favourite book (see photograph page 45).

Illuminate letters.

Illustrate to fit a detailed text (poems work well for this).

Help to design an aesthetic environment for the school library.

Study lettering styles.

DRAMA AND IMAGINATIVE PLAY

Improvisation and role play using favourite stories, poems and plays (either published works, or written by the children).

Make a puppet theatre.

Set up a library desk in the reading corner with relevent equipment. Children record issued and returned books.

ASSEMBLY

Talk about the purpose, importance and use of the library: include the fact that books are borrowed, not bought, and the implications of this.

Use the children to act out the life of a book, from the author's first idea to its place on a bookcase.

Books and Stories

How a Book is made by Aliki, Hippo Books.

A Visit to the Library by Althea, Cambridge University Press.

On the Way Home by Jill Murphy, Picture Mac.

Poems and Rhymes

'Summing Up' in *School's Out*, compiled by John Foster, OUP.

'Billy Dreamer's Fantastic Friends' in *Gargling with Jelly* by Brian Patten, Penguin.

Songs and Music

Sing a Story, A & C Black.

'The Three Bears', *Okki Tokki Unga*, A & C Black.

'Gobbolino The Witch's Cat', *Appuskidu*, A & C Black.

Canals and Waterways

> **Reflections**:
> Fold the paper in half. Paint the outline of a scene with a boat on the top half in black paint and fold over; open out and paint in the areas in the top half with colour. Fold over periodically to print, before the paint dries. You may need to touch up areas which are too dry to print.
>
> **Roses and Castles**:
> Using reference from books, ideas and objects, show how traditional art of canal boat painting was carried out – then let the children try it for themselves.

Stimulus
A visit to a canal or waterway.

LANGUAGE

Collections
Photographs and posters of boats and life on waterways.
Word resource bank.

Samples of traditionally painted canal ware.
Brochures and leaflets of waterway holidays.
Word resource bank.

Discussion
Who has had experience of waterways?
What is the difference between a canal, a river and a stream?
Why are waterway holidays so popular?

Activities

Write a brief history of the canal system: why it began; how it was built and run; early life on the working canals.

Compare life of a child on a working narrow boat (as part of a large family), and life of a child on a holiday narrow boat these days.

Design and write brochures and leaflets to advertise a modern canal boat hire company.

Discuss advantages and disadvantages of working and living on a boat.

Make a comparison between life in a house and on board a boat and/or life in a town, and life on a waterway.

Write poems describing the tranquility and peace of a waterway.

Write in a journalistic style of a river or canal accident e.g. running aground, getting stuck in a lock, etc.

Write 'wanted' posters for people who vandalise or mistreat the waterways (in the early days of canals, punishment was quite severe!)

Write about a day in the life of a waterways horse, written in the first person.

MATHEMATICS

Collection

Price lists of holiday hire boats.
A retractable tape measure.
A selection of measuring bowls.
Plasticine.
Small waterproof objects, e.g. Lego.

Discussion

How much is it to hire a 2/3/4 berth narrow boat? How much for one week/two weeks in summer and winter? Why does the price change?

How many children would like to have a holiday on the waterways?

Activities

Group in sets for early multiplication, e.g. '3 boats with 2 people on each – how many people altogether?'

Transfer the above to block graphs and discuss the sizes of jumps.

Produce block graphs or pictograms to record results of surveys into favourite types of holidays, to include canal holidays.

SCIENCE

Collections

Water play equipment.

Plasticine.

Pulleys, levers, scrap wood, string.

Recyclable materials e.g. cereal packets.

Photographs of locks and bridges.

Reference of waterway wildlife.

Discussion

How do canals go uphill without the water running away? Introduce the theory of locks.

How do people get across the canal? Discuss the need for bridges of different types, include swing bridges and raising bridges.

How are boats powered in modern times?

The natural life of canals: birds, insects and minibeasts, plants.

Pollution and litter and its effect.

Why does the water in canals not soak away?

Activities

Experiment with the waterproof quality of clay: does it hold water when wet, dry, painted, varnished?

Find out what happens when clay is left soaking in water.

Design and build a swing bridge, working on a pivot of some kind.

Design and make a raising bridge.

Using recyclable materials, make a model of a lock system.

Identify wildlife seen on the waterway and carry out a survey.

Investigate the plant life.

Go 'pond dipping' in the waterway, under strict supervision.

Investigate how space is saved through furniture design. Design and make collapsible tables, drop-down beds etc.

Using water trays, experiment with floating and sinking: which objects float, which sink? Can you make a 'floater' sink and a 'sinker' float?

Find out how many objects a 'floater' will carry before it sinks (Lego, bricks, beads etc). Does it depend on the size of the floater?

SOCIAL SCIENCES

Discuss the reclamation of the canal system. Why is much of it in a state of disuse? Talk about the Industrial Revolution, and the great days of the canals.

Study the canal system on maps.

ART AND CRAFT

Study the traditional canal boat decorations and paint roses and castles

Use the designs to paint objects e.g. wooden spoons, boxes, tins etc.

Make traditional lace plates, by punching holes around paper plates, threading ribbon through and drawing a picture in the centre.

Practise block writing own names and introduce the use of a dropped shadow.

JADE

Make 3D model boats.
Paint symmetrical reflection paintings (see photograph).
Try painting wet on wet, wet on dry, and dry on wet. Compare the results.
Do close observational drawing of plants found along the waterway.
Design and paint posters for canal holiday companies.

DRAMA AND IMAGINATIVE PLAY
Explore working together in small confined spaces.
Mime sailing through a lock.

ASSEMBLY
Discuss the way families lived in the working canal boats; the need to work together, sharing responsibilities. Compare jobs children did then, and the jobs asked of them now e.g. tidying their bedroom.

Books and Stories
The Cow who fell in the Canal by Phyllis Krasilovsky, Picture Puffin.
Where the River begins by Thomas Lockyer, Patrick Hardy Books.
Canals, Ladybird Books.

Poems and Rhymes
'Reflections' in *Cadbury's Sixth Book of Children's Poetry*, Beaver Books.
'Legging the Tunnel' in *Second Poetry Book*, OUP.

Songs and Music
'On the River Flows' in *Flying a Round*, A & C Black.
'Row, Row the Boat' in *Flying a Round*, A & C Black.
'Rosie', Tom Stanier, *Watch* (BBC), Macdonald Educational.

Fairgrounds

Background:
Blue paper with green foreground.
Roller coaster: yellow painted strip with base made by printing, using black paint and the edge of a ruler. The carriages are made from nets of boxes, decorated and assembled with people cut out and glued inside.
Foreground:
Paintings of rides, stalls and people.
The Carousel:
Cardboard horses, coloured and cut out and stuck on to decorated 'poles' (strips of card). The roof is constructed from half an old hoop hung from strings, with a cardboard pelmet attached and stapled to the wall. The horses' poles are then attached to that.
Roundabouts:
The 3D models are based on a decorated paper plate, to which is glued an empty cotton reel. A short piece of dowelling is inserted into the centre, and on the top is balanced a decorated cone of card for the roof. Animals or vehicles are drawn, cut out and glued on to striped paper straws, which are then attached to the roof.

Stimulus
The arrival of a fair nearby.
Visit to a fair when it is closed.
A television programme or story.

LANGUAGE
Collection

Photographs and posters of fairgrounds to include the specialist lettering and pattern designs.
Word resource bank.

Discussion

Who has been to the fair?

What is their favourite ride?

Why do people enjoy them so much?

The history of fairs.

The names of the rides and sideshows.

A compilation of words offered by the children to describe the sights, sounds and atmosphere of the fair.

The advantages and disadvantages of belonging to a travelling fair.

Activities

The excitement of the fair lends itself to alliterative, onomatopœic poetry and synonyms.

Write the copy for a poster advertising the coming of a fair (see photograph).

Write adjectives and nouns in pairs of balloons.

Make and write in 'fortune' tellers.

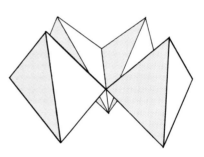

Write acrostic poems using 'fairground' as the frame.

Story writing: The Ghost Train

                After the Fair Had Gone

                I Had £5 to Spend at the Fair

Practise handwriting to decorate the rides.

Play memory language games based on 'I went to the fair and I had a ride on the . . .'

Find and use recipes for ice cream, hot dogs, pop corn and toffee apples. Draw cartoon strip showing sequence of activity when cooking.

MATHEMATICS

Collection

Commercially produced, and home made, fairground type games e.g. hoopla, bagatelle (see Art and Craft).

A wide assortment of price labels and numbered stickers for games.

Discussion

Ordinal numbers: who went on first, second etc?

Would the children prefer a charge on the gate and free rides, or a payment for each activity?

Is a trip to the fair value for money? What else could you do/buy for that amount of money?

Activities

Draw plan views from the top of the Big Wheel.

Make board games.

Practical sharing: 'If Daddy bought 8 toffee apples for 4 of us, how many would we have each?'

Base work: 'There are 13 people waiting for the Waltzer. 3 can go into each carriage and there are 4 carriages. Draw a picture to show what happens.'

Play target games (Aunt Sally, hoopla etc.) and keep score.

Play shove ha'penny.

Experiment with pattern making as used in fairground decorations.

Use calculators to investigate repetitive addition when scoring.

Calculate the cost of families visiting the fair e.g. If the roundabout costs 50p for adults and 20p for children, how much would it cost for 3 children and their mother to have a ride?

As above, but calculate the cost of fairground food e.g. candyfloss.

SCIENCE

Collections

Bottle tops, elastic bands, cotton reels, bulbs, crocodile clips, wire, batteries.

Any old pieces of machinery containing cogs, e.g. a bicycle.

Discussion

What makes the fair so attractive at night?

How are the lights and rides powered?

Introduce basic vocabulary connected with machinery e.g. levers, pulleys, cogs, switches.

Study bulbs and batteries closely.

Activities

Investigate ways to light a bulb. Can you light two bulbs from one battery? A progression of skills can be encouraged by producing a set of tasks, stored in individual boxes, with the challenge clearly written out, and the necessary equipment in the box.

Investigate using switches.

Use a selection of items to sort sets of conductive and non-conductive materials.

Make a circuit with coloured bulbs to light a fairground model (see Art and Craft).

Using cardboard cogs and/or cotton reels, investigate how cogs work.

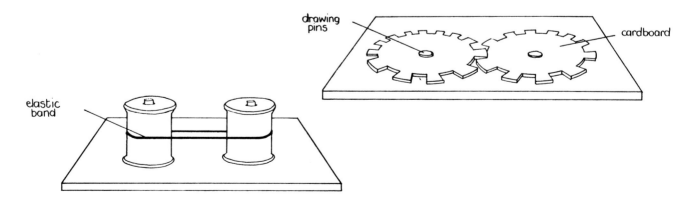

Design and make a game using a prescribed set of equipment e.g. 2 bean bags, 12 bricks and a skipping rope.

Build a helter-skelter to roll a marble down.

Design and make some form of turning or spinning game.

ART AND CRAFT

Design a poster advertising a fair, with maximum visual impact (discuss lettering size and style, images, essential information etc).

Design tickets.

Investigate the 'pouncing' technique, where a picture is traced and holes are pricked along the outline. It is then laid on to the paper on which it is to be painted and a fine powder (talc, chalk dust etc.) is puffed through the holes using cotton wool or soft brush. When the tracing paper is removed, the outline can be seen as little dots, which can be joined up.

Paint traditional fairground decorations.

Traditional lettering.

Wax resist night-time fairs.

Make 3D models of trailers and lorries.

Make 3D fairground food.

Drawings and collages of electrical circuits, batteries and bulbs.

DRAMA AND IMAGINATIVE PLAY

Mime 'crowd' movements.

Pretend you are getting lost in a crowd.

Act out movements connected with individual stalls: eating sticky candyfloss, riding on the dodgems, being scared on the ghost train etc.

Juggling.

Make up sound stories, using voices and percussion to simulate the excitement of the fair.

Set up food stall selling imitation toffee apples, hot dogs, burgers, candyfloss.

Books and Stories
Angelina at the Fair by Katharine Holabird, Picture Puffin.
My Naughty Little Sister at the Fair by Dorothy Edwards and Shirley Hughes, Little Mammoth.
Going to the Fair by Heather Amery and Peter Wingham, Usborne Simple Readers.

Songs and Music
'Animal Fair' in *Okki Tokki Unga*, A & C Black.
'I've got a Lovely Bunch of Coconuts', Trad.
'Scarborough Fair', Trad.

Parks

Stimulus

A visit to a local park and its nursery, if possible.

A visit by a park keeper to the school.

LANGUAGE

Collections

Seeds, seed packets, bulbs (if in season).

Bedding plants, compost, pots, basic gardening tools (large and small).

A selection of different soils.

Word bank.

Reference books of gardening and landscaping.

Leaflets from parks, and National Trust information.

Maps showing parkland.

Discussion

Where are the local parks?

How would you get there?

Who uses them?

Why do we have parks?

History of parklands in Britain: the involvement with Royalty etc.

Types of parks: national, wild, recreation, leisure, theme etc.

Activities

Interview visitors to a local park. Why do they go there? When do they usually visit? What do they do there?

Interview the people who work at the park.

What games can be played in a park? Invent some new ones taking into account specific features of the local park e.g. trees, hills, buildings.

Consider safety aspects: don't go with strangers; what to do if you are approached.

Make a survey of the facilities: are they enough? If relevant, write to the Parks Manager with suggestions for improvements.

Compare the park by day and night: is it locked by night? If so, why?

Write a brochure advertising the park.

Describe the park from the viewpoint of a bird/baby/elderly resident/mother.

Write about 'A Year in the Life of a Park' – through the seasons.

Compile a questionnaire to send to local residents concerning the park.

Use photographs taken by the children as stimulus to caption writing and reporting.

Look at rules in the park. What are they? Do you agree with all of them? What rules would you add/omit?

An Exhibition of Flower Paintings.

Background:
A chequered pattern of two colours complimentary to the paintings.

Mounts:
Black borders, mounted onto one of the above two colours. Alternate the colours to display.

Paintings:
Use cartridge paper and drawing inks (water based). Always have direct stimulus of the flowers, and encourage really close and accurate observation. Draw preliminary rough sketches in order to understand the flower structure, arrangements in the vase etc. Use old saucer or mixing palettes and pour a little ink into them. Dilute with water to obtain lighter tones. Inks produce beautiful effects when they run together: otherwise, allow them to dry first, as you would with paints.

MATHEMATICS

Collections

Maps, specifically of parks, and general maps.

Details of opening hours of the local park.

Aerial photographs.

Discussion

Maps and plans of the park.

Co-ordinates and plotting, to be developed into a game like battleships.

Draw together, and decide on suitable methods of recording, the information gained from surveys and questionnaires (see Language).

Hours of opening – how long is the park open in summer/winter etc?

Activities

Design an adventure playground using solid shapes.

If the park has a tea shop, set up a cafe in the classroom as a money handling activity.

Draw rows and columns of flowers (beginnings of multiplication).

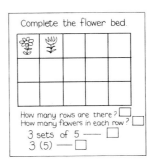

Complete the flower bed.

How many rows are there? ☐
How many flowers in each row? ☐
3 sets of 5 — ☐
3 (5) — ☐

Design flower beds using pegboards, showing symmetrical patterns.

Record and measure seedling/bulb growth.

Draw plans to investigate area, using squared paper. How many squares does the pond cover? How long is the car park etc?

SCIENCE

Collections

Seeds and bulbs.

Magnifying equipment.

Houseplants.

Soil samples.

Reference books on plants and insects.

Gardening tools, large and small.

Discussion

What do plants need to grow?

What habitats do certain animals need?

How does the weather affect the park?

Ecology, conservation and the problem of litter.

Activities

Design a wheelbarrow after studying an example of one, and questioning a gardener as to the essential features.

Experiment with growing conditions using fast growing seeds e.g. cress, bean sprouts. Cover some with a cone of black paper; deny some water etc.

Examine and compare seeds and bulbs.

Conduct soil sample experiments.

Identify trees and flowers, and name parts.

Study root structure of plants: re-pot the class houseplants.

Make compost using food waste – a long-term activity!

Test biodegradability of a variety of materials. Include paper, plastic and glass.

Make a wormery and discuss the value of worms in the garden.

Talk about the food chain.

Make a wildlife study of birds, small mammals, domestic pets who use/live in the park: recognition surveys, feeding habits etc.

Base sand or water tray work on the boating pool or sand pit in the park.

Design a park to suit people's particular requirements i.e. children, the disabled, senior citizens, teenagers, pet owners.

Make a miniature park and playground with working models (see photograph).

Take cuttings from easily cultivated plants.

ART AND CRAFT

Make 3D flowers in tissue and crêpe paper.

Design and construct miniature gardens.

Use vegetable and fruit prints to build up flower beds.

Make paper chain flowers by folding paper concertinas and cutting flowers out through all the layers.

Make close observational drawings and paintings of plants.

Design an anti-litter poster for the park.

Cut a print of Van Gogh's 'Sunflowers' into 6 or 8 pieces, give a piece to each group of children and ask them to paint it accurately on a large piece of paper, then piece the large paintings together to make a huge reproduction.

Welcome to Jellystone!

Background:
Maps designed and drawn by the children to include features they regard as important in a park. 'Rules' devised by the children, with illustrated borders.

Model:
On the base of hardboard, the 'grass' is made of soap flakes mixed with warm water and green paint, to a mouldable consistency. It is then landscaped on the base, and left overnight to dry. Playground equipment is made from dowelling, balsa wood, string, card, recyclable materials – the children design it on paper first. The people are made from pipe cleaners and material scraps.

DRAMA AND IMAGINATIVE PLAY

Act out a confrontation between a park keeper and a group of wrong-doers.

Mime activities which go on in the park.

Set up a tea shop based on one in the park.

ASSEMBLY

Each child prepares a speech, looking at the park from a different viewpoint e.g. child, dog, flowers, mother, jogger, etc. Stress the interdependence and responsibilities of all involved.

Books and Stories
Alpaca in the Park by Rosemary Billam, Picture Lions.
The Park in the Dark by Martin Waddell, Walker Books.
When we went to the park by Shirley Hughes, Walker Books.

Poems and Rhymes
'The Bossy Young Tree' in *Gargling With Jelly* by Brian Patten, Penguin.

Songs and Music
'English Country Garden' in *Harlequin*, A & C Black.
'Let It Be' in *Tinderbox*, A & C Black.
'Tidy Song' in *Tinderbox*, A & C Black.

Theatre

Stimulus
A visit to the theatre.
A visit by a theatre group for performance and/or workshop at the school.
A tour of the local theatre, i.e. backstage, to include dressing rooms, scenery etc.

LANGUAGE

Collection
Theatre posters, programmes and tickets.
Puppets, to include glove, shadow, marionettes.
Books of plays.
Dressing-up clothes, preferably unusual,
for character work and role play.
Don't forget to include accessories such
as shoes, bags, hats, scarves, bow ties,
feather boas etc. N.B. multicultural,
non sexist.

Face paints.

Word resource bank.

Discussion
What is the theatre? How is it different from television and cinema?
Who has been to the theatre?
What sort of plays have you seen? Pantomimes? Comedy? Drama?
Discuss vocabulary: set, scenes, acts, understudy etc.
The role of actors and actresses: it is a job, and they go home afterwards!
Comparisons between theatre, television, films, real life.
Other people involved in the theatre: producer, director, choreographer, properties manager, house staff etc.
If possible, invite an actor or actress to talk to the children.
Terminology of the theatre building e.g. stalls, balcony, boxes.

Activities
Using the story of the history of the theatre, introduce to the children selected examples of historical plays e.g. the chorus in Greek tragedy, Shakespeare.
Investigate the history of theatre-going.
Write plays.
Summarise plays you have seen.
Study story structures: plays need a beginning, middle and a satisfying ending.
Read plays to an audience: the children need to be aware of the importance of clarity and expression.
Following the above activity, write reviews of the plays seen performed by friends.
Character development: study the part played by one character in a play.
Make flow charts tracing the events in the play. This could either be written or drawn.
Re-tell the story of a play, perhaps changing the ending or one of the characters.
Draw events in the play as 'stills' to teach the correct
usage of speech bubbles and thought bubbles.

Again, draw events in the play as 'stills', but with the speech written below to teach the children the use of speech marks.

A large painting could be made of a scene, and the children could choose from a selection of pre-written speech bubbles and glue them beside the appropriate characters to tell a story. This could also be done on a felt or magnet board.

Describe the characters created by the use of make-up – use face paints to create different characters (be aware of stereotyping).

Following a study of a programme from the theatre, the children could write autobiographies or biographies for inclusion in a class book.

Talk/write about the advantages and disadvantages of being a famous actor or actress.

Autograph writing: the children could design their own signature and invent short sayings to go with them. Have a book in which to collect autographs.

Describe the effects of lighting.

MATHEMATICS

Collections

Prices and tickets from box offices.

Collection of empty boxes and bags of sweets (boxes can contain beans, bags can contain polystyrene pieces).

Discussion

How much does it cost to go to the theatre? Why do we have to pay?

If your trip involves coach/train fares, the children can be involved in pricing the trip. How long will it take to get there?

Why are there intervals? How long do they last?

Activities

Seat prices: are they value for money?

Set up a sweet/ice cream shop for the interval.

Time: calculate the length of a performance, the interval, and the journey time.

SCIENCE

Collection

Levers and pulleys.

Equipment to make electrical circuits.

A selection of materials and fabrics.

Discussion

Why do theatres have a fire curtain?

Should anything else be made from fire-proof materials?

How are curtains and scenery raised and lowered?

Discuss the need for lighting in the theatre.

Activities

Fireproof and test materials.

Work with levers and pulleys to raise and lower objects. These could be incorporated into a large model theatre, to enable scenery to be changed, to open and close curtains or to make mechanism for special effects such as trapdoors.

Make circuits to light model theatres, to include coloured lighting effects, and spotlights.

Work with sound: make model megaphones. Do they change the volume of speech?

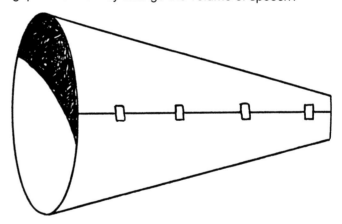

ART AND CRAFT

Make model theatres.

Make puppets.

Make masks.

Face painting – create characters. The children could then draw their portrait, working from a photograph of themselves with make-up on (see photograph).

Design costumes.

Design and make props.

Paint scenery using rollers, sponges, diffusers, stencils, large decorating brushes.

Design posters advertising plays.

DRAMA AND IMAGINATIVE PLAY

Set up a play reading area in the classroom/hall.

Set up a dramatic play area for a pretend theatre, with free access to dressing-up clothes, with books and pictures for stimulus.

Devise direct drama and mime from the play the children saw.

Portray characters through the use of voice/movement.

Toshi drew herself made up as Little Red Riding Hood!

Photograph of a child in stage make-up, portraying a character from a play or story, perhaps as part of a production or a 'Book Week' activity: the child uses the photograph to draw a portrait of himself/herself as accurately as possible. Display the photos and drawings side by side.

Books and Stories
Albert & Albertina by Colin and Moira Maclean, Arrow Books Ltd.
Prince Cinders by Babette Cole, Picture Lions.
Tanya Loved to Dance by Satomi Ichikawa, Picture Puffin.
The Almost Awful Play by Patricia Reilly Giff, Picture Puffin.

Poems and rhymes
'My Sister Betty' by Gareth Owen in *Song of the City*, Young Lions.

Songs and Music
'The Clown', *Appuskidu*, A & C Black.
'There's No Business Like Show Business', *Classic Irving Berlin*, Chappell.

Parental/Adult involvement

At the beginning of the school year, some teachers find it useful to have an informal chat with their new parents, perhaps over a cup of tea, to introduce themselves, talk about their methods of working, make any requests for equipment and materials, and to ask for helpers. Following this, another meeting for those offering their time and energy is helpful, to sort out which subject areas people wish to work in, and to arrange mutually suitable times. It might be useful to have a duplicated sheet with a list of suggested activities for parents so that they can decide at their leisure how they can help.

When working with parent helpers, it is essential to brief them thoroughly about the task in hand:–
The standard of work you expect from the children.
The length of time each group should be with them.
The need for open-ended questioning and investigative work.
The aim of the activity – what the children should achieve.
The fact that their role is to assist and supervise – the work should be done by the children.
Any clearing up should be done by the children.

Remember! You are in charge, and the standards and activities should be set by you.

It is usual for the teacher to set up the activity and provide the necessary equipment and written instructions. Any training or explanation should take place before the beginning of the teaching session! Below is a suggested list of activities in which parents could become involved.

Within the school – with children
Cookery
IPA
Reading – sharing books, telling stories
Educational games
Language activities
Art and Craft
Investigative Maths and Science work
Issuing books and running the library
Computer
Gardening
Technology
Games and P.E.
Musical activities
Going on outings
Acting as scribe – writing or typing children's stories as they tell them
Photography

Within the school – classroom management
Keeping painting/creative area clean and well-stocked
Mending and sorting reading/library books
Mounting work, preparation of caption strips and covering pinboards
Making books and folders of different sizes
Sharpening pencils and crayons

At home
Mending and making role-play clothes
Covering and painting storage boxes
Adapting and painting furniture
Taping stories
Typing children's stories from written work

Organisation of Outings

Preliminary Visit

When deciding on a place to visit for a school trip, it is essential to make a preliminary visit. During this time, it would be helpful to check the following:–

The best route, method of transport, cost and time of journey.

The opening and closing times.

Parking arrangements.

If going by coach, where the dropping off/meeting points would be.

If going by public transport, both the journey time and the time taken to walk to and from the station/bus stop.

Location of toilet and First Aid facilities.

Whether there are any special services offered e.g. worksheets, guided tours, slide shows, feeding times etc.

Where coats and lunch bags may be left.

Where lunch would be eaten in wet/fine weather.

The shop is the highlight of the trip for some children, and prices should be checked in order to establish the amount of pocket money the children may bring. Also there may be a need for restrictions in size of groups allowed in the shop due to lack of space.

Notes made during the preliminary visit can be used to produce worksheets for the children to complete during the visit. If suitable, in order to alleviate boredom during a long journey, an 'I Spy' game is useful.

Booking

When making a booking, check the group booking rates on both admission and fares. The cost of accompanying adults may need to be shared out and incorporated in the children's price per head.

In the letter to parents informing them of the trip and asking for contributions towards the cost, the following may need to be mentioned:

Date and place of visit.

Time and place of return/departure.

Method of transport.

Maximum amount of pocket money (if wished) in a named purse.

Suitable clothes and footwear.

Food provision: if packed lunches are to be taken, they are best brought in carrier bags, so that everything can be thrown away – no bottles!

Do not forget to include a request for relevant information about medical conditions: travel sickness, hay fever, allergy to animals etc.

At the end of the letter should be a detachable permission slip, to include a request for parent helpers, if needed:–

'I can/cannot accompany this visit.'

Parent Helpers

Parent helpers are essential and invaluable to most trips. The smaller the adult/child ratio, the more the children benefit, and the more the adults enjoy themselves!

Once the number of adults has been established, the children need to be grouped accordingly. This should be done before the morning of the trip, and each member of the group could be given a name and label with its own colour or motif. Ensure that each child knows the adult in charge of his/her group and vice versa.

'Parent packs' containing the following are greatly appreciated by most helpers:

A short letter thanking the parents for coming, and 'briefing' them about what you would like the children to have done and seen – vital for follow up work.

A simple itinerary giving times of arrival, departure, lunch etc.

A map, if relevant, showing toilets, lunch area, meeting points.

Clipboards for their group, with attached worksheet(s).

Pencils, rubbers, sharpeners.

Spare paper.

Tissues.

A list of the names of the children in their group.

On the Day

Hold a short 'settling down' talk and 'briefing'. Be sure that the children know what to do should they get lost. Check that all the children have brought their lunches in disposable bags, and that their purses are either in safe, fastening pockets or given to the adult in charge of their group (not in the lunch bag – it will end up being thrown away!).

The following would prove useful:–

A bucket lined with a plastic bag (plus spares) for travel sickness.

A roll of kitchen paper.

A change of clothes.

A small First Aid kit.

A plastic bottle of water.

A supply of sweets to suck for the journey.

A camera.

Have a wonderful day!

For details of further Belair publications,
please write to:

BELAIR PUBLICATIONS LTD.,
P.O. Box 12,
TWICKENHAM
TW1 2QL,
England.